D1606496

GLOW YOUR WORTH

Affirmation & Gratitude Journal to Ignite Unconditional Love

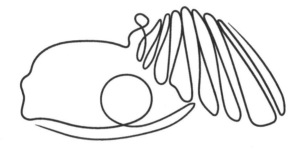

SONIA DE FAZIO

First paperback edition October 2021
Published by bSocial Communications Inc.

Book design by Valerie Damen
Illustrations by Valerie Damen

ISBN 979-8-4898-5097-1 (paperback)

www.glowyourworth.com
www.glowyourworth.ca

Written and designed in Edmonton, Alberta.

Lined and designed by Valerie Damen.

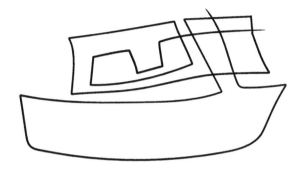

Dedicated to all the healers who helped me sail out to sea.

SHE FOUND HER SOUL
BY THE SEASHORE

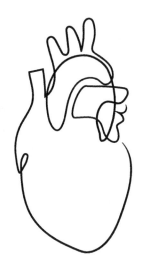

When I finger through my Rolodex of childhood memories, I can pinpoint the first moment I experienced unconditional love: sitting on damp sand, with my hair dreadlocked into crispy curls from the seaweed scented mist of the ocean's salty abyss.

Immediately upon touching my toes to scorched sand, I knew I was home. I ran into the water so quickly as if I were demanding baptism. The water was more than inviting, it was necessary. It was the breath in my lungs, the rhythm that fed my heart.

I was immersed in a solitary rendezvous with sunshine and sea, with a newfound sense of belonging to the waves. I trusted the ease in the push and pull of the water. I surrendered to its infinity; its uncertainty, polarity and power. There was something about the combination of land, sea and sun that felt spiritual and peaceful.

Whatever this force was, I was a part of it too. I knew my connection ran deep. It was pure bliss and happiness. My heart was full. Just as I was. Me and sea.

This was a big moment for my little seven year-old heart. My heart and sea became my identity. Speaking of...

At the tiny age of two, I was sent to the Stollery Children's Hospital, in prairie-patched Alberta, for heart surgery. A heart valve that typically finds a way to close on its own was stubborn enough to stay open in mine. A rolling, gurney-type bed too big to comfort my tiny frame transported me into a blindingly frigid room to face the adult-like reality I had to encounter at such a young age. I had to trust someone else with my heart.

Even with this sense of vulnerability and fragility, I still lived my little years with my heart wide open. I was visceral and vibrant, easily excited by the sight of a craft table piled high with pipe cleaners and pom poms. I was completely content enjoying the simple pleasures of my life, eating chalky Fun Dip candy, watching disjointed Ren and Stimpy episodes, and cruising around on my blue banana-seat bike. I was always ready to give it all I had to make someone, anyone, smile and laugh, in an effort to share the joy that overflowed within me. It wasn't uncommon to see me claim any flat surface as an imaginary stage to passionately perform my choreographed rendering of "It's a beautiful life! Oh, oh, oh!" Completely unsolicited.

I thrived when it came to matters of the heart; creativity, connection, communication and caring for others. Always giving generously and compassionately with no expectation of receiving anything in return. I loved everyone. I loved me.

I remember my girlhood vividly, as if it were a silent, grainy clip from an old film that will forever be projected on my memory. Nostalgia became an untouchable relic, a profound piece of history, showcasing the power and purity of my uninhibited, gregarious love. Digging up these sentimental, youthful memories reminds me that a love like this does exist and that living in this capacity, with my heart wide open, is safe to do.

I can't recall the exact moment when that unbridled love for myself took a spot on the back burner, but as I'm sure most of us experience, it happened gradually, over time. My journey, my dreams, my desire to connect authentically with the universe and others, my self-love all dropped to the bottom of my priority list.

Over time, I fell into the unhealthy habits of over-giving and overextending myself all in a selfish attempt to receive and feel love from the people around me. Giving all my love away without extending any of that love back to myself slowly whittled away at my self-worth. Each time I stayed silent instead of expressing my emotions, hid away my creative essence or put other people's emotional needs above my own, a bit of self-love flaked away from my heart, leaving me depleted and empty.

Unconditional love was ripped from the hands of my soul and put into the hands of other people. I looked to others to give me the happiness, belonging, validation and acceptance I was craving. I believed that I was only worthy of love when the people around me were happy and satisfied.

Through this act of giving my love away, I began a collection. I traded Pogs, Beanie Babies and Sailor Moon cards for barricades to my worthiness. I collected "unworthy blockages" that slowly, over time, pulled me farther and farther away from feeling worthy of loving myself. I would have rather had the pop culture crazed collectables.

Instead, I stocked up on reasons why I wasn't worthy:

- Pumping the brakes on my energetic, quirky personality, because it wasn't acceptable or conducive in a desk-bound society.

Blockage #1 — "I'm unworthy of expressing myself."

- People pleasing, saying "yes" even when I didn't want to, not being able to freely express my thoughts or feelings, over-giving in non-reciprocal relationships.

Blockage #2 — "I'm unworthy of healthy boundaries."

- Constant self-doubt, making decisions based on external influence instead of going with my gut, feeling directionless and lost with no sense of purpose.

Blockage #3 — "I'm unworthy of trusting my intuition."

- Believing I needed to make a certain amount of money to be happy or that a certain salary range would show that I'm good at my job. That it would be too hard to make money running my own business full-time. Believing I had to work hard to be successful.

Blockage #4 — "I'm unworthy of abundance."

- Being completely blindsided with tragic news that abruptly ended a twelve-year relationship with someone I thought was my best friend and life partner. Enduring the unsettling disruptions that come along with going through a divorce.

Blockage #5 that felt more like a worthy wreckage — "I am unlovable."

By my barely-early thirties I found myself going through a divorce, moving homes and going in for surgery. At the same time I was opening my eyes from a morphine slumber, I was receiving a slew of text messages from friends informing me of school closures and toilet paper hoarders. COVID was on the rise. Darkness and devastation clouded the minute amount of optimism and faith I had left. Isolation forced me into solitude. Solitude forced me into silence. Silence provoked my thoughts. My thoughts consumed me.

Love did not exist for me anymore. The way I spoke to myself was destructive and debilitating. "I'm a failure, I'm incompetent, I'm inadequate, I don't belong anywhere," were a recurring refrain that I shared with myself. The amount of water left in my well was equivalent to an evaporated teardrop. I felt completely empty and worthless. I wasn't worthy of showing myself love and compassion because I didn't feel worthy of anything.

That agonizing sadness cracked me right open and forced me into hermit mode. I sat with the pain, and took the space and time to feel it all the way through. While this process was incredibly uncomfortable, the intense, polarizing pain somehow dispatched a Bat-Signal to that little firecracker, who was still tagging along with me. My inner child put down the imaginary microphone from singing Ace of Base to shout out "there is something better than this."

When I leaned in and turned up the volume on my internal chatter, I saw the negative, destructive, guilt-riddled, limiting dialogue that plagued me for years. It was a spiral staircase of societal norms, familial expectations, mindless meanderings of judgment and fears. I was drenched in a narrative of outcomes that I was either holding onto from the past, or worries of the future that were not even in my current reality.

I was held captive by my thoughts, ripping me away from my freedom of living in the moment. I finally acknowledged the power and polarity of my words.

I realized that if my thoughts could be this dark and restrictive, they also have the capacity to be light and expansive.

I could see the direct correlation between my thoughts and feelings, and the reality I found myself living in. My outer world was mirroring my inner emotional state. I had to make a choice. To either stay stagnant in this pattern of self-hatred, or to finally forgive and learn to love myself. I knew I had to give myself the compassion, praise and validation that I needed and to take a firm stance in believing that I was worthy of healing. I was finally ready to use my tenacity and strength to explore my self-worth and to allow myself to shine bright and take up space in this world. This was my mission. I would stop at nothing.

To overcome my blockages, I filled my physical and mental space with positive and powerful self-love affirmations. Worthy words and expressions of gratitude were my new musical composition. I lined pages with affirmations that filled journals brimming with bits of encouragement, cover to cover, stacked with poetic prophecies that I would read back to myself with allegro. I collected empowering affirmations that created a colourful motif of tiny boxes that were scattered around my apartment.

This empowering self-love practice became my tethering point. In moments of doubt and spiralling internal criticism, I sat with my thoughts, accepted them without judgement, and spoke to myself with love. Gratitude breathed life into my words. Feeling appreciation for who I was and what I had transmuted my lyrics of self-sabotage into a love song.

Gratitude and affirmations were the séance, the ritual that connected me to my soul. I am brought back to the "sea of the crime," that memorable moment of love, when the sea shared a whisper with me.

Love washes over me. Like the sea shares a blanket of water to warm the shore, words of worthiness comfort me in times of pressure. I feel the power of the cosmos when it mirrors the moon and ocean waves. I feel love for my journey and the magic I create in this world. I feel compassion and passion growing in my heart, to authentically connect with everyone and everything.

I am forever grateful for that whisper I received by the sea. Now, I know and glow, I am worthy of love. I am worthy of being me.

THE GLOW YOUR WORTH JOURNEY

Worthiness is at the core of who you are. It is being "good enough," an intuitive understanding that you have value and that you deserve to have value. You are worthy because you're a unique, powerful presence on this earth, with gifts, passion and purpose that only YOU have. Self-worth is your personal journey and connection to worthiness.

Having self-worth is loving yourself, unconditionally. It's the internal sense of being enough, now. Even in moments of change and disruption, you can still feel worthy of living the life you love. When you feel worthy of loving yourself, you have the capacity to love others just the same, free from judgment, control and expectations.

The *Glow Your Worth* journey will empower you to go inward to love yourself so much that it will naturally ignite your intuitive sense of self-worth. *Glow Your Worth* will encourage you to use affirmations and gratitude to transform negative and limiting self-talk into empowering thoughts. The book will invite you to nourish positive thoughts and take inspired action toward joy and happiness.

By removing "unworthy blockages" you will begin to speak more compassionately to yourself. Affirmations and gratitude will replace criticism with encouragement, validation and love. When you speak kindly to yourself and accept the beauty of your imperfection, you build a narrative and mindset that is abundant and loving. With an abundant mindset, you'll know that you are enough. You'll be able to dig deep and uncover what makes you unique and what makes you shine, and then bring that passion to life, with excitement!

Consistent use of positive "I am" affirmations will elevate and encourage your mind to have empowering self-talk. Affirmations can be used anytime you need them. You can speak them out loud in the mirror as you admire your beauty. You can use affirmations as a mantra in meditation or write them out when you're journaling. Affirmations are simple and short so you can remember and use them as a placeholder when your thoughts fall into the habit of holding you back.

When you think from love, you will begin to feel and act from love. Daily gratitude paired with affirmations will encourage you to integrate your uplifting narrative and transform it into emotions and feelings. Spoken and written words of appreciation are the light force and energy that that will allow you to feel your self-worth.

Self-worth feels boundless. As you begin to build self-worth, it will feel like you're living in a flow state, with so much clarity, drive and excitement. You will feel balanced in your emotions and have the strength and happiness to get through any situation, regardless of the outcome.

Thinking, feeling and acting from unconditional love and self-worth is what will connect you to self, creative source and selfless love. When you are moving through the world as your most authentic self, and know you have great purpose in doing just that, you burn a bright light that shines within you and around you.

Because when you know your worth, you *Glow Your Worth*.

MY INTENTION AND
HOPE FOR YOU

Glow Your Worth is a collection of soulful affirmations I wrote and spoke to myself while exploring my own self-worth healing journey. These words inspired, encouraged and empowered me to love with an open heart. My intention is to encourage you to reach for more positive, loving and compassionate thoughts to feel worthy of following your joy.

I hope that what helped open my heart will help expand yours enough to feel the power and peace of being in alignment with worthiness. I hope these words will encourage you to adventure back to a time when you felt the purest source of love and worthiness, when you were open to play, exploration and creative expression, and to feel that sense of worthiness again. Your self-worth is already within you. You just have to remember what it feels like.

Your journey to healing isn't linear. This book isn't intended to be either. *Glow Your Worth* doesn't have to be traditional "front to back" book experience. It's your journey, your words of gratitude and your love. I want you to trust your intuition and follow what you feel you need for growth and healing. Feel through the words and pick each affirmation as you wish. Take as much time as you need with each affirmation and go through each page, in any order.

Allow your energy and intuition to guide you to what you need at this moment. Be guided by the words, illustrations, numbers and what comes to you when you put pen to paper. Trust that pull. Trust divine timing. Trust that you are exactly where you need to be. This book is in your hands for a reason.

1

I am enough.
What I say is enough.
What I do is enough.
What I have is enough.
Who I am is enough.

I am grateful for...

_____

_____

_____

_____

_____

_____

_____

_____

_____

_____

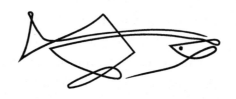

2

I allow my soul to decide my path.
I am worthy of following what feels good to me.
I follow what brings me bliss and joy.
I follow the passions that ignite my heart.

I am grateful for...

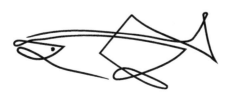

3

I am a powerful creator.
I radiate with love, from the inside out.
My energy is powerful.
I have the power to raise the frequency of the whole universe.

I am grateful for...

4

I courageously step into my truth.
I release guilt, shame and fear.
I confidently communicate my choices.
I am grateful for my voice.

I am grateful for...

_____

_____

_____

_____

_____

_____

_____

_____

_____

_____

5

I open my heart to gratitude.
I feel my heart being filled with appreciation and acceptance.
I notice my thoughts transform when my focus is positive.
The more gratitude I feel, the more abundance flows in.
I am grateful.

I am grateful for...

_____

_____

_____

_____

_____

_____

_____

_____

_____

6

My purpose is perfect.
My worthiness is pure.
My love is unconditional.
My creativity is abundant.
My adventures are limitless.

I am grateful for...

_____

_____

_____

_____

_____

_____

_____

_____

_____

7

I am forgiving.
I forgive myself freely.
I am compassionate towards my friends and family.
I grow more patient with others by forgiving myself.

I am grateful for...

_____

_____

_____

_____

_____

_____

_____

_____

_____

_____

_____

8

I am worthy of belonging.
I am supported by my community.
I am abundant in love and community.
I am grateful for all my connections.

I am grateful for...

_____

_____

_____

_____

_____

_____

_____

_____

_____

_____

_____

_____

_____

9

I am worthy of peace.
I am floating on a boat of calm in waters of uncertainty.
I seek out balance and harmony.
Inner peace is my reality.

I am grateful for...

_____

_____

_____

_____

_____

_____

_____

_____

_____

_____

10

I embody my inherent power.

I am meant to be a powerful source of abundance.

The way I manifest prosperity and wealth is by aligning my purpose with service to others.

I know how I can best serve my community.

I am grateful for...

11

I bathe in the beauty of life.
Calm washes over me when I embrace the now.
I am always creating.
I am whole.

I am grateful for...

_____

_____

_____

_____

_____

_____

_____

_____

_____

_____

_____

12

I practice mindfulness.

In moments of bliss, I ground in the present and appreciate what I have.

In moments of pain, I accept and know it will pass.

I am grateful for all my emotions and experiences.

I am open to receiving it all.

I am grateful for...

_____

_____

_____

_____

_____

_____

_____

_____

_____

_____

13

I make space for expansive happiness.
My vulnerability opens my heart to unconditional love.
I give and receive love freely.
I am worthy of living in love.

I am grateful for...

_____

_____

_____

_____

_____

_____

_____

_____

_____

_____

14

I am a deliberate creator.
I choose my thoughts.
I choose my actions.
I am my reality.

I am grateful for...

15

Today, I give myself the gift of imperfection.
The only thing I ask of myself is to progress.
Perfection is not my journey.
Perfection doesn't exist for anyone.
I am enough.

I am grateful for...

_____

_____

_____

_____

_____

_____

_____

_____

_____

_____

16

I am willing to feel all my pain and transmute it into love.
My love is powerful.
My love is divine.
I am love consciousness.

I am grateful for...

17

I am magic.
I alchemize dark into light.
I choose my thoughts.
I write the script to my reality.
I live the life I love.

I am grateful for...

_____

_____

_____

_____

_____

_____

_____

_____

_____

_____

18

I am grateful for the ordinary.
Beautiful, simple pleasures fill my day.
Embracing simplicity ignites my authenticity.
I am worthy of all my blessings.

I am grateful for...

_____

_____

_____

_____

_____

_____

_____

_____

_____

_____

19

I am my soul.
My soul is patient.
My soul is happy.
My soul is whole.
My soul is expansive.

I am grateful for...

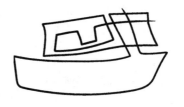

20

I am grounded in the present moment.
I release attachment to outcomes.
I am worthy of enjoying my journey.
I am exactly where I need to be.

I am grateful for...

_____

_____

_____

_____

_____

_____

_____

_____

_____

_____

_____

_____

_____

21

I am worthy.
I am worthy, simply because I am here experiencing life.
My worthiness is not attached to any outcome.
My worthiness is not attached to any person.
I am whole and complete.

I am grateful for...

_____

_____

_____

_____

_____

_____

_____

_____

_____

_____

22

I am authentically me.
My thoughts, feelings and actions are all aligned.
I am grateful for my integrity.
My integrity is a magnet to prosperity and joy.

I am grateful for...

_____

_____

_____

_____

_____

_____

_____

_____

_____

_____

23

I love myself boldly and honestly.
I admire my ability to accept all of who I am.
I am excited to show my authentic self to the world.
I love all of me.

I am grateful for...

24

I am worthy of enjoying the simple things.
I approach the day with excitement and curiosity.
I allow my inner child to roam free.
I am worthy of being present in play.

I am grateful for...

_____

_____

_____

_____

_____

_____

_____

_____

_____

_____

_____

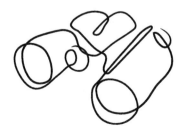

25

I am worthy of forgiveness.
I love how freely I forgive others.
I love how easily I forgive myself.
My heart is as light as a feather.

I am grateful for...

_____

_____

_____

_____

_____

_____

_____

_____

_____

_____

_____

26

I am worthy of being my most authentic self.
I inspire others by just being me.
I inspire myself when I speak my truth.
My authenticity is magnetic.

I am grateful for...

_____

_____

_____

_____

_____

_____

_____

_____

_____

_____

_____

_____

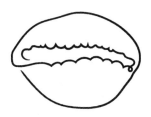

27

I am worthy of trusting my intuition.
When something doesn't feel right, I listen.
When something feels right, I listen.
The more I trust my intuition the louder it gets.
My intuition is always truthful.
I am grateful for my inner voice.

I am grateful for...

_____

_____

_____

_____

_____

_____

_____

_____

_____

28

I am worthy of vibrating at my highest energy.
I am thriving in my own energy.
I intentionally think, feel and act from a place of love.
My vibration is high and is radiating off my soul.
My energy is aligned with peace, joy and love.

I am grateful for...

_____

_____

_____

_____

_____

_____

_____

_____

_____

_____

29

My words create my reality.
I speak my truth.
I express myself freely.
I don't take external responses personally.
My words vibrate with love.

I am grateful for...

_____

_____

_____

_____

_____

_____

_____

_____

_____

_____

30

My purpose is sacred.
I honour who and what I am.
I am intentional.
I am purposeful.
I am.

I am grateful for...

_____

_____

_____

_____

_____

_____

_____

_____

_____

_____

_____

31

My soul's journey travels along with many other souls.
We each take the leading role in our own story.
My story is one that I am writing for myself.
I love watching my journey unfold.

I am grateful for...

_____

_____

_____

_____

_____

_____

_____

_____

_____

_____

32

I release resistance.
I understand that wanting is resistance.
I understand that not wanting is resistance.
I am open to what is meant for me.

I am grateful for...

33

I am love.
My courage is love.
My strength is love.
My kindness is love.
My vulnerability is love.

I am grateful for...

_____

_____

_____

_____

_____

_____

_____

_____

_____

34

I am patient with my process.
I am kind to myself.
I feel the emotions I need to feel.
I speak to myself with compassion.
I welcome my emotions with gratitude and let them in with ease.
I am grateful for my growth.

I am grateful for...

35

I dance to the rhythm of my highest vibration.
I allow my body, mind and soul to appreciate the now.
I let go of expectations and live in this dance.
I take one step at a time.
My dance is beautiful.

I am grateful for...

_____

_____

_____

_____

_____

_____

_____

_____

_____

_____

36

I am worthy of allowing my emotions to flow.
I accept my emotions as they are.
I accept my emotions in the form they come.
I acknowledge what I am thinking and feeling.
I wholeheartedly love all my emotions.

I am grateful for...

_____

_____

_____

_____

_____

_____

_____

_____

_____

_____

37

I am worthy of my beauty.
I detach my self-worth from my appearance.
I am more than just my body and image.
I focus on my internal beauty.
I nourish my body with love.
I am beautiful.

I am grateful for...

_____

_____

_____

_____

_____

_____

_____

_____

_____

_____

_____

38

I am meant for victory.
There is no need to rush the process.
I am here to enjoy the journey.

I am grateful for...

_____

_____

_____

_____

_____

_____

_____

_____

_____

_____

_____

_____

39

I am worthy of embracing change.
Circumstances shift in my favour.
I allow what is meant for me to flow in with ease.
I surrender to clarity and transformation.
I trust the process.

I am grateful for...

_____

_____

_____

_____

_____

_____

_____

_____

_____

_____

_____

40

I am worthy of living a life I love.
I am worthy of happiness.
I am worthy of passion.
I am worthy of pleasure.

I am grateful for...

_____

_____

_____

_____

_____

_____

_____

_____

_____

_____

_____

41

I am awake.

I am aware.

Everything I see in the world is a reflection of me.

I accept my reality.

I am open to healing.

I am grateful for...

_____

_____

_____

_____

_____

_____

_____

_____

_____

_____

42

I am worthy of feeling content.
I am worthy of opening my heart to support and stability.
My heart beats to the rhythm of miraculous abundance.
I am abundant.

I am grateful for...

_____

_____

_____

_____

_____

_____

_____

_____

_____

_____

43

The greatest journey I take is inward.
Here, I make friends with my inner child.
I tune in with my intuitive compass.
I feel the essence of my soul.
I see the purpose of my creation.
I already hold all the answers to life.

I am grateful for...

_____

_____

_____

_____

_____

_____

_____

_____

_____

_____

_____

44

What crashes and burns is reborn again.
Growth and destruction exist in balance.
I need the darkness to experience the light.
I embrace the duality of my existence.

I am grateful for...

_____

_____

_____

_____

_____

_____

_____

_____

_____

_____

_____

_____

45

I am worthy of telling my story.
I heal through the vibration of my voice.
I heal through singing my pain.
I heal through expressing my emotions.
I heal through speaking kind words to myself.
My words heal.

I am grateful for...

_____

_____

_____

_____

_____

_____

_____

_____

_____

46

I am worthy of living the life I love.
I create my own rules.
I create my own limitations.
I create my happiness.
My dreams can be my reality.

I am grateful for...

_____

_____

_____

_____

_____

_____

_____

_____

_____

_____

47

I ask for what I want.
I say my intentions out loud with excitement.
Let it be heard by the divine.
My words are alive.
They breathe life into my destiny.

I am grateful for...

_____

_____

_____

_____

_____

_____

_____

_____

_____

48

I fearlessly express myself.
I experience freedom through my words.
I tell my story with excitement.
I use my words to heal myself and others.

I am grateful for...

_____

_____

_____

_____

_____

_____

_____

_____

_____

_____

49

I surrender to the sweetness of life.
I love to play.
I love to explore.
I love to create.
I am grateful for all my adventures.

I am grateful for...

_____

_____

_____

_____

_____

_____

_____

_____

_____

_____

_____

50

I am worthy of living in the moment.
I enjoy the simplicity of this present moment.
I feel the essence of my soul.
I am present.

I am grateful for...

_____

_____

_____

_____

_____

_____

_____

_____

_____

_____

_____

_____

51

My words create positive change.
My story heals.
My song connects me to others.
My voice is sacred.
I am worthy of sharing my story.

I am grateful for...

_____

_____

_____

_____

_____

_____

_____

_____

_____

52

I am worthy of taking a leap of faith.
Infinite possibilities exist outside my comfort zone.
I lean into moments of discomfort.
Under pressure is when I experience expansive growth.
I am grateful for my courage.

I am grateful for...

_____

_____

_____

_____

_____

_____

_____

_____

_____

_____

53

I am worthy of having an open heart.
I release limiting beliefs.
I let go of control.
I am open to all the possibilities beyond my comprehension.

I am grateful for...

_____

_____

_____

_____

_____

_____

_____

_____

_____

_____

54

I am worthy of acceptance.
When I accept others, I learn to fully accept myself.
I accept who I am.
I am enough.

I am grateful for...

_____

_____

_____

_____

_____

_____

_____

_____

_____

_____

55

I am worthy of being enough.
The most precious opportunity I have on this earth is being me.
I embrace my journey.
I am powerfully authentic.

I am grateful for...

_____

_____

_____

_____

_____

_____

_____

_____

_____

_____

56

I am worthy of abundance.

I surrender to prosperity.

I surrender to success.

I surrender to the ease and stability that comes with an abundant mindset.

I am grateful for...

_____

_____

_____

_____

_____

_____

_____

_____

_____

_____

57

I am worthy of my existence.
No one is less or more important than I am.
I release external expectations.
I release the expectations I force on myself.
I am free to be me.

I am grateful for...

_____

_____

_____

_____

_____

_____

_____

_____

_____

_____

58

I am worthy of all my lessons.
My experiences help me build resilience, strength and grace.
My suffering is balanced with abundance, love and peace.
I am open to receiving it all.
My lessons are blessings.

I am grateful for...

_____

_____

_____

_____

_____

_____

_____

_____

_____

_____

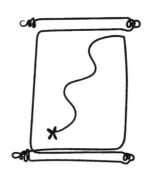

59

I am worthy of forgiveness.
I speak to myself with love and compassion.
I accept the person I am today, not the person I might be.
I am perfect in my imperfection.

I am grateful for...

_____

_____

_____

_____

_____

_____

_____

_____

_____

_____

60

I am worthy of exploration.
I connect to my heart by connecting to my inner child.
When I play and explore, I feel my heart exploding with wonder.
I feel empowered and liberated when I express myself creatively.

I am grateful for...

_____

_____

_____

_____

_____

_____

_____

_____

_____

_____

_____

61

I am worthy of love.

People come into my life for a reason.

I embrace these relationships and accept all lessons.

I accept that when I feel rejection, I am being redirected to something better.

I am on the right path.

I am grateful for...

_____

_____

_____

_____

_____

_____

_____

_____

_____

_____

_____

62

I am patient with my growth.

The seeds I've planted are comfortably nestled in the universe's energetic soil.

My seeds are nourished with the water and light I feed them, every day.

I embrace the liberation of divine timing.

I am grateful for...

_____

_____

_____

_____

_____

_____

_____

_____

_____

_____

_____

_____

63

I am my own home.
I feel centred within myself in any environment.
I do not act based on people's opinions and judgements.
My thoughts and actions belong to me.

I am grateful for...

_____

_____

_____

_____

_____

_____

_____

_____

_____

_____

_____

64

I am consistent with building healthy habits.
My routine allows me to heal and be my best self.
I release limiting habits and thoughts.
I let go of people and situations that are no longer aligned with me.
I am grateful for my healing.

I am grateful for...

_____

_____

_____

_____

_____

_____

_____

_____

_____

_____

_____

65

I am open to all my experiences.
I accept all memories and moments equally.
I don't bypass my challenges.
I am grateful for all my lessons.

I am grateful for...

_____

_____

_____

_____

_____

_____

_____

_____

_____

_____

_____

_____

66

Rejection is an opportunity for me to have my own back.
I love myself no matter what.
I am whole and complete as I am.
I am worthy of love.

I am grateful for...

67

I fill my well with love.
All my emotional needs are met.
I am safe.
I am loved.
I belong.
My voice is heard.
My light is seen.

I am grateful for...

_____

_____

_____

_____

_____

_____

_____

_____

_____

68

I live life with grace.
I choose ease.
I choose forgiveness.
I choose faith.
I choose gratitude.
I choose compassion.

I am grateful for...

69

I am mastering my most authentic self.
I follow joy and happiness.
I show up ready to be unapologetically who I am.
I love showing off my vibrant personality.

I am grateful for...

_____

_____

_____

_____

_____

_____

_____

_____

_____

_____

_____

70

I deserve to walk away.

I walk away from what is no longer in alignment with who I am.

I walk away with genuine intention, not as a strategy of manipulation.

This is how I love myself and build healthy boundaries.

Walking away is love.

I am grateful for...

71

I am worthy of shining bright.
I shake things up.
I express myself freely.
I shine a light on what is dull, dark and stagnant.
I am a liberated force.

I am grateful for...

_____

_____

_____

_____

_____

_____

_____

_____

_____

_____

_____

72

I can open my heart fully because I'm meant to feel it all.
I am safe to feel fear and pain.
I am safe to feel joy and pleasure.
I am safe to feel.

I am grateful for...

_____

_____

_____

_____

_____

_____

_____

_____

_____

_____

_____

_____

73

My authenticity glows when I follow my heart.
The joy I feel is enough.
The happiness I feel is enough.
The passion I feel is enough.
I am whole and complete.

I am grateful for...

_____

_____

_____

_____

_____

_____

_____

_____

_____

_____

_____

_____

_____

74

I am worthy of being seen.
By being vulnerable, I create a safe space for others to do the same.
My authenticity is my grandest gift.
I allow the world to see me as I am.

I am grateful for...

75

My love is enough.
Being myself is enough.
My own validation is enough.
What I have is enough.
Where I am is enough.
I am enough.

I am grateful for...

_____

_____

_____

_____

_____

_____

_____

_____

_____

76

I am worthy of forgiveness.
I forgive myself for not expressing my boundaries.
I forgive myself for holding onto resentment.
I forgive myself for being consumed by destructive thoughts.
I forgive myself, wholeheartedly.

I am grateful for...

_____

_____

_____

_____

_____

_____

_____

_____

_____

_____

_____

77

I am worthy of having fun.
I love entertaining my inner child.
I play, explore, and laugh.
I have the freedom to be curious.
I am inspired to create something new.

I am grateful for...

78

I am mastering the rhythm of balance.

I flow through cycles of my life with compassion and ease.

I feel my heart and mind work together in harmony.

I am grateful for the light and dark in all stages of my development.

I am grateful for...

_____

_____

_____

_____

_____

_____

_____

_____

_____

_____

79

My passion is power.
I cherish the fiery passion within myself.
I bring it to life and watch it spread happiness like wildfire.
My passion is divinely rewarded.

I am grateful for...

_____

_____

_____

_____

_____

_____

_____

_____

_____

_____

_____

80

My day is painted with possibility.
My life is coloured with beautiful surprises.
I am open to receiving all my miracles.
I am grateful for my blessings.

I am grateful for...

_____

_____

_____

_____

_____

_____

_____

_____

_____

_____

_____

_____

_____

81

I am abundant in happiness.
I am abundant in laughter.
I am abundant in adventures.
I am abundant in creativity.
I am abundant in playfulness.
I am abundant in joy.
I am worthy of abundance.

I am grateful for...

_____

_____

_____

_____

_____

_____

_____

_____

82

I am worthy of having free will.
I choose my thoughts.
I choose how I react to others.
The only validation I seek is from myself.
I trust my decisions.

I am grateful for...

_____

_____

_____

_____

_____

_____

_____

_____

_____

83

I am worthy of rest.
I deliberately take time for self-care.
I treat myself with compassion.
I give myself grace.

I am grateful for...

_____

_____

_____

_____

_____

_____

_____

_____

_____

_____

_____

_____

_____

84

I dance with destiny.
Together, we co-create love and light.
What is mine will always find its way to me.
I trust in divine timing.

I am grateful for...

_____

_____

_____

_____

_____

_____

_____

_____

_____

_____

_____

_____

85

I am worthy of moving into the light.
I release self-judgement.
I release self-sabotage.
I release unnecessary expectations of myself.
I release limiting beliefs that no longer serve me.

I am grateful for...

_____

_____

_____

_____

_____

_____

_____

_____

_____

_____

86

I love who I have grown into.
I acknowledge and celebrate my healing.
I am worthy of loving myself for all that I am.
I am enough.

I am grateful for...

_____

_____

_____

_____

_____

_____

_____

_____

_____

_____

_____

87

I am courageous.
I am resilient.
I am kind to myself.
I have the strength to heal.

I am grateful for...

_____

_____

_____

_____

_____

_____

_____

_____

_____

_____

88

I am a beaming light of positivity.

I put my best self forward in all my interactions.

I choose to act from a space of kindness, compassion and forgiveness.

I am worthy of sharing my light with the world.

I am grateful for...

_____

_____

_____

_____

_____

_____

_____

_____

_____

_____

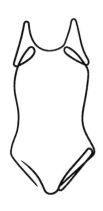

89

I am worthy of forgiveness.
I forgive those who put their pain on me.
I forgive myself for not letting go sooner.
I allow compassion to flow through me.
I am grateful for my healing.

I am grateful for...

_____

_____

_____

_____

_____

_____

_____

_____

_____

_____

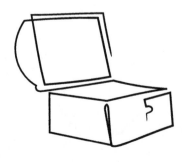

90

I am the moments in between.
My life is not about the beginning or end.
I am this moment.
I am now.

I am grateful for...

_____

_____

_____

_____

_____

_____

_____

_____

_____

_____

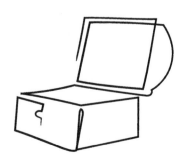

91

I am deeply connected to my imagination and intuition.
Emotions and creativity flow through me.
I nurture what brings me love and happiness.
I allow my heart and passion to guide me.

I am grateful for...

_____

_____

_____

_____

_____

_____

_____

_____

_____

92

I am not stuck.
I am experiencing new thoughts.
I am experiencing new feelings.
I am experiencing new energy.
I am open to new experiences.

I am grateful for...

93

My heart is open.
Love flows through me with ease.
Beauty flows through me with ease.
Gratitude flows through me with ease.

I am grateful for...

_____

_____

_____

_____

_____

_____

_____

_____

_____

_____

_____

_____

_____

94

I am worthy of unconditional happiness.
Happiness is already within me.
Happiness is my natural state.
Sharing joy and happiness is my purpose.

I am grateful for...

_____

_____

_____

_____

_____

_____

_____

_____

_____

_____

_____

_____

_____

_____

_____

95

I surrender to the unknown.
The void is where all possibilities and opportunities are created.
I feel at ease when I accept all outcomes.
I trust my journey.

I am grateful for...

96

I have an abundant mindset.
I think from abundance.
I act from abundance.
I speak from abundance.
All my senses are grounded in abundance.

I am grateful for...

_____

_____

_____

_____

_____

_____

_____

_____

_____

_____

_____

_____

_____

97

I am worthy of my words.
I give my words life by speaking my truth.
I open up the bridge between my heart and my voice.
I glow a bright light the more I express my purpose.

I am grateful for...

_____

_____

_____

_____

_____

_____

_____

_____

_____

_____

_____

98

My path is mine to walk.
What is meant for me will always be mine.
I replace expectation with acceptance.
I am grateful for where I am.

I am grateful for...

_____

_____

_____

_____

_____

_____

_____

_____

_____

_____

_____

_____

99

I am worthy of my blessings.
I surrender to wealth.
I surrender to success.
I surrender to divine timing.
Abundance is my birthright.

I am grateful for...

_____

_____

_____

_____

_____

_____

_____

_____

_____

_____

100

I am worthy of peace.
My day unfolds as it's meant to.
My mind and emotions are at ease.
I live today with a fully inspired heart.

I am grateful for...

_____

_____

_____

_____

_____

_____

_____

_____

_____

_____

101

I honour and respect my lessons.
Regardless of the outcome, my path will always be mine.
I am on the path to my highest potential.
I celebrate my growth.

I am grateful for...

_____

_____

_____

_____

_____

_____

_____

_____

_____

_____

102

I am an infinite source of energy.
I choose to think, feel and act from love.
The energy I radiate into the world is pure and beautiful.
My glowing, positive energy comes back to me tenfold.

I am grateful for...

_____

_____

_____

_____

_____

_____

_____

_____

_____

_____

_____

103

I am present.
I find my true essence in stillness.
I watch the world around me.
I am at peace with where I stand within it.

I am grateful for...

_____

_____

_____

_____

_____

_____

_____

_____

_____

_____

104

I am always creating.
There is creation in darkness.
There is creation in the light.
I appreciate and accept the cycles of creation.

I am grateful for...

_____

_____

_____

_____

_____

_____

_____

_____

_____

_____

_____

_____

105

I am worthy of slowing things down.
I respect how I use my energy.
I respect how I use my time.
I don't need to rush the process.
I am patient.

I am grateful for...

_____

_____

_____

_____

_____

_____

_____

_____

_____

106

I choose authenticity.
I choose to let myself be seen.
I choose to let myself be heard.
I choose to be grateful.
I choose joy.

I am grateful for...

107

I am worthy of my gifts.
I grow into my gifts through exploration.
I create from love.
I share from love.
My passion is love.

I am grateful for...

_____

_____

_____

_____

_____

_____

_____

_____

_____

108

I am worthy of speaking my truth.
My words are my power.
I tell my story with courage.
I speak from my heart.
I use my words to heal.

I am grateful for...

_____

_____

_____

_____

_____

_____

_____

_____

_____

109

I am worthy of it all.
My potential is limitless.
My opportunities are endless.
My abundance is overflowing.
My love is unconditional.
My dreams are for me to explore.

I am grateful for...

110

My mindset is grounded in abundance.
I generously give from abundance.
I patiently receive abundance.
Abundance is my birthright.
I am abundant.

I am grateful for...

_____

_____

_____

_____

_____

_____

_____

_____

_____

_____

_____

111

I create heaven on earth.
I design my thoughts.
I design my feelings.
I design my actions.
I paint my path with intention.

I am grateful for...

_____

_____

_____

_____

_____

_____

_____

_____

_____

_____

112

My purpose is pure.
I bathe in the beauty of my soul.
I cleanse myself of limiting beliefs.
I cherish my purpose.

I am grateful for...

113

My passion is compassion.
Following my purpose ignites happiness within me.
My joy opens my heart to unconditional love.
My passion warms the hearts of others.
My love heals.

I am grateful for...

_____

_____

_____

_____

_____

_____

_____

_____

_____

_____

114

I am my own home.
I am thriving in my own space and energy.
I come to myself for love and care.
Everything I need is right here.

I am grateful for...

_____

_____

_____

_____

_____

_____

_____

_____

_____

_____

115

I am present.
I am experiencing all of life right now.
By living in the moment, I open the door to my full potential.
I am worthy of my existence.

I am grateful for...

_____

_____

_____

_____

_____

_____

_____

_____

_____

_____

116

I love how much I love.
My emotions are beautiful.
My empathy is pure.
My heart is the sun.
It lightens the day and welcomes the night.
I am love.

I am grateful for...

_____

_____

_____

_____

_____

_____

_____

_____

_____

_____

117

My soul is one of a kind.
I love that I don't fit in.
I love that I stand out.
I love that I take up space in this world.

I am grateful for...

_____

_____

_____

_____

_____

_____

_____

_____

_____

_____

118

I am worthy of my journey.
I am always growing and learning, in all circumstances.
The opinions of others don't sway me from being my best self.
I love who I am.
I love my journey.

I am grateful for...

_____

_____

_____

_____

_____

_____

_____

_____

_____

_____

_____

119

My soul intuitively trusts the universal bond of connection.
I simply am.
You simply are.
We are all connected.

I am grateful for...

_____

_____

_____

_____

_____

_____

_____

_____

_____

120

I am worthy of keeping my heart open.
I am open to receiving all that I am.
I am open to receiving all that I deserve.
I am open to receiving all the blessings and miracles available to me.
I am open to receiving positive energy.
I am open.

I am grateful for...

_____

_____

_____

_____

_____

_____

_____

_____

_____

121

I am worthy.
I am my most powerful self when I validate my own worthiness.
My worth is not determined by what other people think of me.
Their words and thoughts are part of their story, not mine.
I create my own worthiness.

I am grateful for...

_____

_____

_____

_____

_____

_____

_____

_____

_____

_____

122

I am worthy of compassion.
I treat myself with compassion.
I listen to my thoughts with compassion.
I speak to myself with compassion.
I experience change with compassion.

I am grateful for...

_____

_____

_____

_____

_____

_____

_____

_____

_____

_____

123

My life is filled with endless possibilities.
I enjoy all the surprises delivered to me, big and small.
I am showered with magic and miracles.
I am open to receive all my blessings.

I am grateful for...

_____

_____

_____

_____

_____

_____

_____

_____

_____

124

I am a multidimensional creature.
I love all that I am.
I love all that I feel.
I allow my soul to expand.

I am grateful for...

_____

_____

_____

_____

_____

_____

_____

_____

_____

_____

_____

_____

125

I am worthy.
I am worthy of having my heart held.
I am worthy of honesty and loyalty.
I am worthy of stability.
I am worthy of love.

I am grateful for...

_____

_____

_____

_____

_____

_____

_____

_____

_____

I am beautiful.

My confidence is beautiful

My courage is beautiful.

My compassion is beautiful.

My love is beautiful.

I am grateful for the beauty I bring into this world.

I am grateful for...

127

My joy is limitless.
I make space for expansive happiness.
I bathe in the beauty of bliss.
I am happy.

I am grateful for...

_____

_____

_____

_____

_____

_____

_____

_____

_____

_____

128

I am worthy of listening to my body.
When my body tells me to rest, I rest.
When my body tells me to meditate, I meditate.
When my body tells me to get up and move, I move.
I am intuitively connected to my body and know what it needs.

I am grateful for...

_____

_____

_____

_____

_____

_____

_____

_____

_____

_____

_____

_____

129

Perfection is not my purpose.
Making mistakes is how I learn and grow.
My lessons are stepping-stones to my highest potential.
My mistakes are beautiful.

I am grateful for...

_____

_____

_____

_____

_____

_____

_____

_____

_____

_____

_____

130

I am an eternal soul.
My purpose is to experience life.
My dreams are for me to explore.
I am grateful for following my heart.

I am grateful for...

_____

_____

_____

_____

_____

_____

_____

_____

_____

_____

_____

_____

131

I am worthy of reclaiming my power.
I am strong.
I am independent.
I am fierce.
I am self-sufficient.
I am powerful.

I am grateful for...

_____

_____

_____

_____

_____

_____

_____

_____

_____

_____

_____

132

I am exactly where I need to be.

I trust in divine timing and allow things to come as they are meant to.

I release timelines.

I release expectations.

I release control.

I feel grounded in the present moment.

I am grateful for...

_____

_____

_____

_____

_____

_____

_____

_____

_____

_____

_____

133

I release attachment.
I release attachment to people.
I release attachment to control.
I release attachment to expectations.
I release attachment to outcomes.
I release attachment to needing certainty.

I am grateful for...

_____

_____

_____

_____

_____

_____

_____

_____

_____

_____

134

I am worthy of opening my heart to unconditional love.
I release blockages.
I release fear of abandonment.
I release past pain.
I am free to love.

I am grateful for...

_____

_____

_____

_____

_____

_____

_____

_____

_____

_____

_____

_____

135

I am connected to my heart.

I remember what excited me when I was a child and live out those dreams today.

I am liberated when I am in flow.

I am liberated when I am having fun.

I feel my heart exploding with wonder.

I am grateful for...

_____

_____

_____

_____

_____

_____

_____

_____

_____

_____

_____

136

I am worthy of receiving abundance.
I am letting go of the weight of the world.
I welcome in the immense power of the boundless universe.
Abundance is always available to me.

I am grateful for...

_____

_____

_____

_____

_____

_____

_____

_____

_____

_____

_____

_____

_____

137

I do not chase, I attract.
What belongs to me will always be mine.
What doesn't belong to me will fall away naturally.
I trust the process.

I am grateful for...

_____

_____

_____

_____

_____

_____

_____

_____

_____

_____

_____

_____

_____

138

I am optimistic.
I believe the best of people.
I believe in having a positive attitude.
I always act from a place of compassion, love and generosity.

I am grateful for...

139

I am the creator of my own reality.
My thoughts become words.
My words become actions.
My actions always come from love.
I receive back what I give.
I am worthy of receiving love.

I am grateful for...

_____

_____

_____

_____

_____

_____

_____

_____

_____

140

I am committed to trusting myself.
I am guided by my wisdom.
I am guided by my experiences.
I am guided by my intuition.
I trust my guidance.

I am grateful for...

_____

_____

_____

_____

_____

_____

_____

_____

_____

_____

_____

141

I look into the deepest, darkest depths of my soul and say, "I love you."

My darkness is beauty.

I don't repress it. I set it free.

I embody the darkness to feel the light.

I am whole and complete.

I am grateful for...

_____

_____

_____

_____

_____

_____

_____

_____

_____

142

My emotions are no longer attached to time.
Feelings from the past can be left there.
Worries about the future are not my reality.
I am grounded in what I feel now.
I accept my emotions in this moment.

I am grateful for...

143

I am worthy of loving my shadow self.
I accept my darkness.
I embody my darkness to fully feel the light.
My soul is whole.

I am grateful for...

_____

_____

_____

_____

_____

_____

_____

_____

_____

_____

144

I am worthy.
I know my worth.
I glow my worth.
I am worthy of it all.

I am grateful for...

145

I am worthy of belonging.
I am surrounded by people who celebrate me.
I let go of those who just tolerate me.
I am worthy of reciprocal, loving relationships.

I am grateful for...

_____

_____

_____

_____

_____

_____

_____

_____

_____

146

I am mastering balance, power and unity.
Balance is the harmony of my masculine and feminine energy.
Power is my inner strength and knowledge.
Unity is connection to everyone and everything.

I am grateful for...

_____

_____

_____

_____

_____

_____

_____

_____

_____

_____

147

I am worthy of being me.
I am excited to show the world exactly who I am.
I own my strengths.
I own my weaknesses.
I come as I am.

I am grateful for...

_____

_____

_____

_____

_____

_____

_____

_____

_____

_____

148

I follow flow.
I embrace the momentum of ease.
I know what feels in alignment with my most authentic self.
I move forward with grace and strength.

I am grateful for...

_____

_____

_____

_____

_____

_____

_____

_____

_____

_____

_____

149

I am worthy of releasing stagnant energy.
All obstacles on my path are removed with ease.
I release all low vibrating energy that no longer inspires me.

I am grateful for...

_____

_____

_____

_____

_____

_____

_____

_____

_____

_____

_____

_____

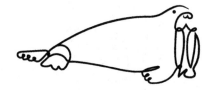

150

I trust in divine timing.

I allow the universe to delight and surprise me.

When I align with bliss, more of that energy will make its way to me.

I am grateful for...

_____

_____

_____

_____

_____

_____

_____

_____

_____

_____

_____

_____

_____

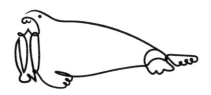

151

I deserve to be authentic.
I embrace my spontaneous nature.
I explore freely and love trying new things.
My authenticity is infinite and always evolving.
Being free is my gift to others.

I am grateful for...

_____

_____

_____

_____

_____

_____

_____

_____

_____

_____

152

I am my number one fan.
I cheer myself on.
I hype myself up.
I remind myself that I am enough.
I am encouraging.

I am grateful for...

_____

_____

_____

_____

_____

_____

_____

_____

_____

_____

_____

153

I am worthy of being optimistic.
I believe the best in people.
I believe the best in myself.
I believe that everything is working out in my favour.

I am grateful for...

_____

_____

_____

_____

_____

_____

_____

_____

_____

_____

_____

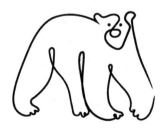

154

What I see in front of me is all happening for me. Not to me.
I accept all outcomes.
I accept all lessons.
The universe has my back.

I am grateful for...

_____

_____

_____

_____

_____

_____

_____

_____

_____

_____

_____

_____

_____

155

I create my own love.
All the love I need is already within me.
I am enough.
I am whole.
I am worthy of loving myself unconditionally.

I am grateful for...

_____

_____

_____

_____

_____

_____

_____

_____

_____

_____

_____

156

My thoughts do not control me.
My internal dialogue is a small part of my consciousness.
I can shift my thoughts at any time.
I choose empowering thoughts.
I am the master of my mind.

I am grateful for...

_____

_____

_____

_____

_____

_____

_____

_____

_____

_____

_____

157

I allow.
I calm the urgency of my ego.
I embrace the patience of my soul.
I find peace in the simple moments.
I am patient.

I am grateful for...

_____

_____

_____

_____

_____

_____

_____

_____

_____

_____

_____

158

Patience is my virtue.
I gently release expectations.
I gently release external validation.
I gently release the hold I have on my past and future self.

I am grateful for...

_____

_____

_____

_____

_____

_____

_____

_____

_____

_____

_____

_____

159

I am worthy of my authenticity.
I admire my unique style and how I express myself.
I am comfortable with how I navigate the world.
I love how I experience life.

I am grateful for...

_____

_____

_____

_____

_____

_____

_____

_____

_____

_____

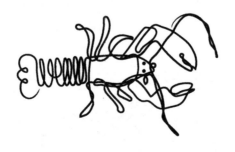

160

My purpose expands beyond my current perspective.
Unexpected changes propel me forward into growth and healing.
I release resistance to change.
I go with the flow.

I am grateful for...

_____

_____

_____

_____

_____

_____

_____

_____

_____

_____

_____

_____

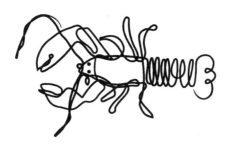

161

I am grounded in my essence.

No matter how much chaos I experience, my spirit is always untouched.

I feel determination glowing in my heart.

I am grateful for my strength.

I am grateful for...

_____

_____

_____

_____

_____

_____

_____

_____

_____

_____

_____

162

I love all my emotions equally.
I accept all my emotions without judgement.
I embrace difficult emotions and allow them to pass.
All my emotions hold purpose.

I am grateful for...

_____

_____

_____

_____

_____

_____

_____

_____

_____

_____

_____

_____

_____

163

My energy is expansive.
I am universal consciousness beyond this physical body.
I am the master of my thoughts.
I am the creator of my reality.
I embrace my greatness.

I am grateful for...

_____

_____

_____

_____

_____

_____

_____

_____

_____

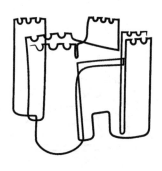

164

I am worthy of listening to my inner inspiration.
My mind is open to new perspectives.
My heart is open to living new experiences.
I am inspired to live the life I love.

I am grateful for...

_____

_____

_____

_____

_____

_____

_____

_____

_____

_____

_____

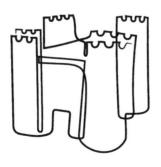

165

I am worthy of living a beautiful life.
I am meant to give generously to others.
I am meant to receive all of life's delicious blessings.
I am grateful for all the prosperity and abundance that surrounds me.

I am grateful for...

_____

_____

_____

_____

_____

_____

_____

_____

_____

166

I am an active participant in divine oneness.
I am connected to everything and everyone.
I see the good in others as they see the good in me.
I am one with love.

I am grateful for...

_____

_____

_____

_____

_____

_____

_____

_____

_____

_____

167

I am worthy of receiving love.
I accept positive comments that are given to me.
I accept the love and compassion of others.
I receive all my blessings with appreciation.
I receive with gratitude.

I am grateful for...

_____

_____

_____

_____

_____

_____

_____

_____

_____

_____

168

I am worthy of my choices.
I choose to live from my heart.
I choose to nourish my mind, body and soul.
I choose positive thoughts.
I choose to heal.

I am grateful for...

_____

_____

_____

_____

_____

_____

_____

_____

_____

169

I am powerfully authentic.
I am here to be who I am meant to be.
The way I take up space is intentional.
My purpose is to be my most authentic self.

I am grateful for...

_____

_____

_____

_____

_____

_____

_____

_____

_____

_____

_____

_____

170

I create heaven on earth.
I transmute all my experiences into pure acceptance.
I embrace life.

I am grateful for...

_____

_____

_____

_____

_____

_____

_____

_____

_____

_____

_____

_____

_____

171

I celebrate the beauty that surrounds me.
The world around me is painted with bright colours.
Each day of healing brings more moments of peace and serenity.
I am grateful for it all.

I am grateful for...

_____

_____

_____

_____

_____

_____

_____

_____

_____

_____

_____

_____

172

I allow the ocean of love to envelop me.
Its embrace is like a warm light on a winter's day.
Unconditional love fills me and overflows onto everyone around me.
I am the purest source of love.

I am grateful for...

_____

_____

_____

_____

_____

_____

_____

_____

_____

_____

_____

_____

_____

173

I play a lead role in my story.
I accept that I play a supporting role in other people's stories.
We come together to mirror each other.
We come together to grow and learn.
I am grateful for everyone who crosses my path.

I am grateful for...

_____

_____

_____

_____

_____

_____

_____

_____

_____

_____

_____

174

I trust the decisions I make for myself.
I do the best with the information I have at this time.
I accept not knowing all the answers.
I move ahead with love and good intentions.

I am grateful for...

_____

_____

_____

_____

_____

_____

_____

_____

_____

_____

_____

_____

175

I am worthy of letting go.
I gently release resentment and anger from my body.
I forgive anyone who has hurt me.
I forgive myself for holding onto this pain as long as I have.
I forgive.

I am grateful for...

_____

_____

_____

_____

_____

_____

_____

_____

_____

_____

176

I am worthy of forgiveness.
I unlock the chains of resentment.
I uplift those who have hurt me.
I love and accept others, exactly as they are.

I am grateful for...

_____

_____

_____

_____

_____

_____

_____

_____

_____

_____

_____

177

I am open.
I openly receive what I need for my soul to grow.
I am awakening my inner guidance.
I have faith in myself.

I am grateful for...

_____

_____

_____

_____

_____

_____

_____

_____

_____

_____

178

I am worthy of letting go.
I accept loss.
I accept change.
Loss opens space for something new to come in.
An abundance of opportunities are already on their way to me.

I am grateful for...

_____

_____

_____

_____

_____

_____

_____

_____

_____

_____

_____

_____

179

I am patient.
I pause to listen to stillness.
I breathe in the calmness of the void.
I trust that things will come together when they are meant to.

I am grateful for...

_____

_____

_____

_____

_____

_____

_____

_____

_____

_____

_____

180

I am worthy of forgiving myself.
I feel lighter by releasing guilt, shame and doubt.
I accept my past, as it was necessary to get me here.
I move forward with compassion.

I am grateful for...

_____

_____

_____

_____

_____

_____

_____

_____

_____

_____

_____

_____

181

I allow.
I surrender.
I cherish.
I embrace.
All of who I am meant to be.

I am grateful for...

182

I am worthy of trusting my inner voice.
I trust my instinct.
I trust my decisions.
I have faith in myself.

I am grateful for...

_____

_____

_____

_____

_____

_____

_____

_____

_____

_____

_____

_____

183

I am blessed when I follow my soul's purpose.
I am rewarded with pure joy.
I am rewarded with love.
I am rewarded with fulfillment.
I am rewarded with abundance and prosperity.

I am grateful for...

_____

_____

_____

_____

_____

_____

_____

_____

_____

_____

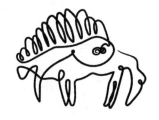

184

I live with childlike wonder and imagination.
I am open to exploring this world and beyond.
I soak up all my experiences.
I love my adventures.

I am grateful for...

_____

_____

_____

_____

_____

_____

_____

_____

_____

_____

_____

185

I am a powerful healer.
I choose to surround myself with positive energy.
I have the strength to transmute negative energy into positive energy.
I am worthy of empowering myself through healing.

I am grateful for...

_____

_____

_____

_____

_____

_____

_____

_____

_____

_____

_____

186

I am designed to dream.
My dreams are unique to my soul's purpose.
My dreams are for me to explore.
I follow my heart.

I am grateful for...

_____

_____

_____

_____

_____

_____

_____

_____

_____

_____

_____

187

I find balance in compromise.
I accept pain and love.
I accept good and bad.
I accept that I am meant to experience polarity.
I accept what is.

I am grateful for...

_____

_____

_____

_____

_____

_____

_____

_____

_____

_____

188

I am worthy of supporting myself.
I motivate myself.
I take action on my goals.
I give myself all the validation I need to follow my heart.

I am grateful for...

_____

_____

_____

_____

_____

_____

_____

_____

_____

_____

_____

189

I am worthy of being grounded.

I breathe in deeply and feel the roots of my feet bury into the core of the earth.

I am safe in this moment.

I am connected to all.

I am grounded.

I am grateful for...

190

I am the purest source of unconditional love.
I love myself without judgement and expectation.
I love my darkness.
I love my light.
I love all that I am.

I am grateful for...

_____

_____

_____

_____

_____

_____

_____

_____

_____

_____

191

I am kind to myself.
I show up for myself, even on the hardest days.
I celebrate my life.
I give myself grace.

I am grateful for...

_____

_____

_____

_____

_____

_____

_____

_____

_____

_____

192

I have an abundant mindset.
I recognize my opportunities are endless.
I share my ideas, gifts and prosperity with love.
I generously give back to my community.
I am abundant because I appreciate what I already have.

I am grateful for...

_____

_____

_____

_____

_____

_____

_____

_____

_____

_____

_____

_____

193

I love myself unconditionally.
I do not put conditions on my love.
I love all my emotions equally, without judgement.
I am a beautiful reflection of my perfect soul.

I am grateful for...

_____

_____

_____

_____

_____

_____

_____

_____

_____

_____

_____

_____

_____

194

I am worthy of cultivating my creativity.
I fill my creative well through play and exploration.
I love sharing my creative gifts with my community.
I am grateful for my creative expression.

I am grateful for...

_____

_____

_____

_____

_____

_____

_____

_____

_____

_____

_____

_____

_____

_____

195

I am worthy.
I am worthy simply because I am here experiencing life.
I am worthy because I choose to be.
I am worthy, right now, in this moment.

I am grateful for...

_____
_____
_____
_____
_____
_____
_____
_____
_____
_____
_____
_____

196

There is expansion in polarity.
The universe is in balance with dark and light.
The darkest moments help grow the brightest days.
I choose to focus on the seeds I've planted through my journey.
I know they will grow into the abundance I've created.

I am grateful for...

_____
_____
_____
_____
_____
_____
_____
_____
_____
_____
_____
_____
_____

197

Miracles come to me when I am in creative flow.
I explore in the beautiful waters of joy.
I float in joy and look up at all the wonders and magic I create.
Joy is where I live.
Joy is where I create.

I am grateful for...

_____

_____

_____

_____

_____

_____

_____

_____

_____

_____

198

I am worthy of success.
I am open to receiving all the abundance that is available to me.
Prosperity and abundance are my birthright.

I am grateful for...

_____

_____

_____

_____

_____

_____

_____

_____

_____

_____

_____

199

I deserve to forgive myself.
I deserve to step away from guilt.
I love myself completely.
I love myself unconditionally.

I am grateful for...

_____

_____

_____

_____

_____

_____

_____

_____

_____

_____

_____

200

I am grateful for my lessons.
I choose to learn, grow and experience all of life.
I choose to see my blessings.
I choose to feel my blessings.
I choose growth.

I am grateful for...

_____

_____

_____

_____

_____

_____

_____

_____

_____

_____

_____

201

I am a wise, magnificent, beautiful individual.
I love myself for who I am today.
I accept that I am no longer the person I was.
I move towards my highest potential.

I am grateful for...

_____

_____

_____

_____

_____

_____

_____

_____

_____

_____

202

When my body tells me to rest, I listen.

I make space for meditation.

I welcome stillness.

I feel peace when I lay down to sleep.

I replenish the beautiful energy needed to recharge my body, mind and soul.

I am grateful for...

203

I choose patience.
I am calm looking into the eyes of the unknown.
I feel at ease with waiting.
I am present in the now.

I am grateful for...

_____

_____

_____

_____

_____

_____

_____

_____

_____

_____

_____

204

I am my soul.
I am without limits.
I am beyond space and time.
I am in everything.
I am the bliss of eternal love.

I am grateful for...

_____

_____

_____

_____

_____

_____

_____

_____

_____

_____

_____

205

I give myself permission to explore.
I follow my inner compass.
I accept my brilliance.
I live fully as my authentic self.

I am grateful for...

_____

_____

_____

_____

_____

_____

_____

_____

_____

_____

_____

206

I love the space around uncertainty.
I release needing control.
I am open to being led by the universe.
I love seeing what shows up for me.

I am grateful for...

207

I am worthy of having uplifting internal dialogue.
I choose to speak to myself with kindness and love.
I choose to replace limiting beliefs with expansive optimism.
I choose to believe in my greatness.

I am grateful for...

_____

_____

_____

_____

_____

_____

_____

_____

_____

_____

_____

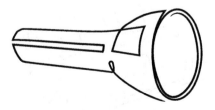

208

I am now.
I am this moment.
I am worthy of this moment.
My presence is valuable.
I treasure my awareness.

I am grateful for...

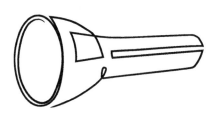

209

I am worthy of opening my heart to love.
I am worthy of loving without conditions.
I am worthy of being loved for who I am.
I am loveable.

I am grateful for...

210

My purpose is to experience life.
I am here to learn and grow.
My life has meaning because I am willing to live it.

I am grateful for...

211

My soul's journey is epic.
Experiences flow through me without resistance.
I surrender to the unpredictability of my path.
I accept it all.

I am grateful for...

_____

_____

_____

_____

_____

_____

_____

_____

_____

_____

212

Peace, love and forgiveness open my heart.

I am open to all the surprises and blessings that will allow my soul to soar.

I am whole and complete just as I am.

I am worthy of living with my heart wide open.

I am grateful for...

_____

_____

_____

_____

_____

_____

_____

_____

_____

_____

_____

213

I am worthy of trusting my intuition.
My intuition teaches me.
My intuition guides me.
I already hold all the answers.

I am grateful for...

_____

_____

_____

_____

_____

_____

_____

_____

_____

_____

_____

214

I am most alive when I am doing what I am meant to do.
I take action in the direction of bliss.
I prioritize my growth and health without guilt or shame.
I am worthy of following joy.

I am grateful for...

_____

_____

_____

_____

_____

_____

_____

_____

_____

_____

_____

_____

_____

_____

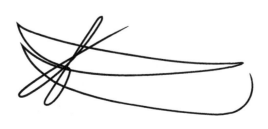

215

I am perfectly imperfect, and I love it.
My heart is open to loving all of my imperfections.
I show up as I am.
I allow the world to see all of who I am.
I am courageous in my vulnerability.
With my hand on my heart, I say "I love all of me."

I am grateful for...

_____

_____

_____

_____

_____

_____

_____

_____

_____

_____

_____

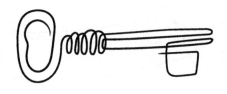

216

I am worthy of belonging.
Standing out is my greatest gift.
Speaking up is my superpower.
I don't seek validation to follow my unique purpose.
I know what is right for me.

I am grateful for...

_____

_____

_____

_____

_____

_____

_____

_____

_____

_____

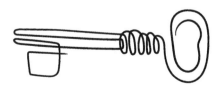

217

I am worthy of my passion.
My passion and purpose are within me.
My passion is my gift to the world.
I express my passion with enthusiasm.

I am grateful for...

_____

_____

_____

_____

_____

_____

_____

_____

_____

_____

218

I am grateful for today.

Even if ordinary, every day holds great potential.

I open myself up to receiving all possibilities by breathing in the moment.

I release all attachment to outcomes.

I am present.

I am grateful for...

_____

_____

_____

_____

_____

_____

_____

_____

_____

_____

_____

_____

219

I am loved by life.
I am loved by the universe.
I am loved by my spirit guides and ancestors.
I am never alone.

I am grateful for...

_____

_____

_____

_____

_____

_____

_____

_____

_____

_____

_____

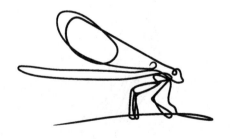

220

I am open.
Love and abundance come together.
This is my reward for following my heart.

I am grateful for...

_____

_____

_____

_____

_____

_____

_____

_____

_____

_____

_____

_____

221

I love courageously.
I love wholeheartedly.
I love with patience.
I love with compassion.
I love the journey of love.

I am grateful for...

_____

_____

_____

_____

_____

_____

_____

_____

_____

_____

_____

222

My abundance overflows onto those around me.
It makes my heart happy when I share with others.
I give with grace.
I give with gratitude.
I give with generosity.
I am abundant.

I am grateful for...

_____

_____

_____

_____

_____

_____

_____

_____

_____

_____

_____

_____

Notes